Not In My Church
Copyright © 2018 by Kyri Demby. All rights reserved.

No part of this publication may be reproduced, stored in retrieval system or transmitted in any way by any means, electronic, mechanical, photocopy, recording or otherwise without the prior permission of the author except as provided by USA copyright law.

This novel is a work of fiction. Names, descriptions, entitles and incidents included in the story are products of the author's imagination. Any resemblance to actual persons, events and entities is entirely coincidental. The opinions expressed by the author are not necessarily those of Demby's Playful Parables

Published by Demby's Playful Parables

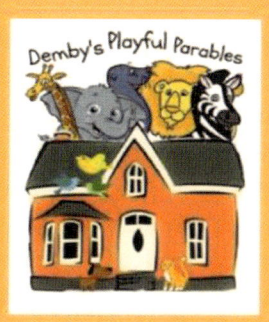

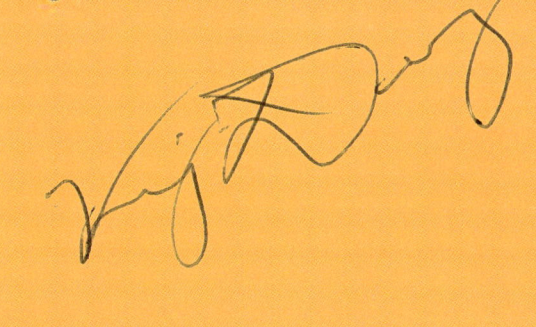

Book design copyright © 2018 by Demby's Playful Parables. All rights reserved.

Cover by Reggie Watkins
Interior Design by Bilal Rasheed
Illustrations by Kimberly James

Published in the United States of America
ISBN: 978-1722707637

Once there was a small, quiet church by a small pond. It was an old country wooden church. For years the families of that small town worshipped there.

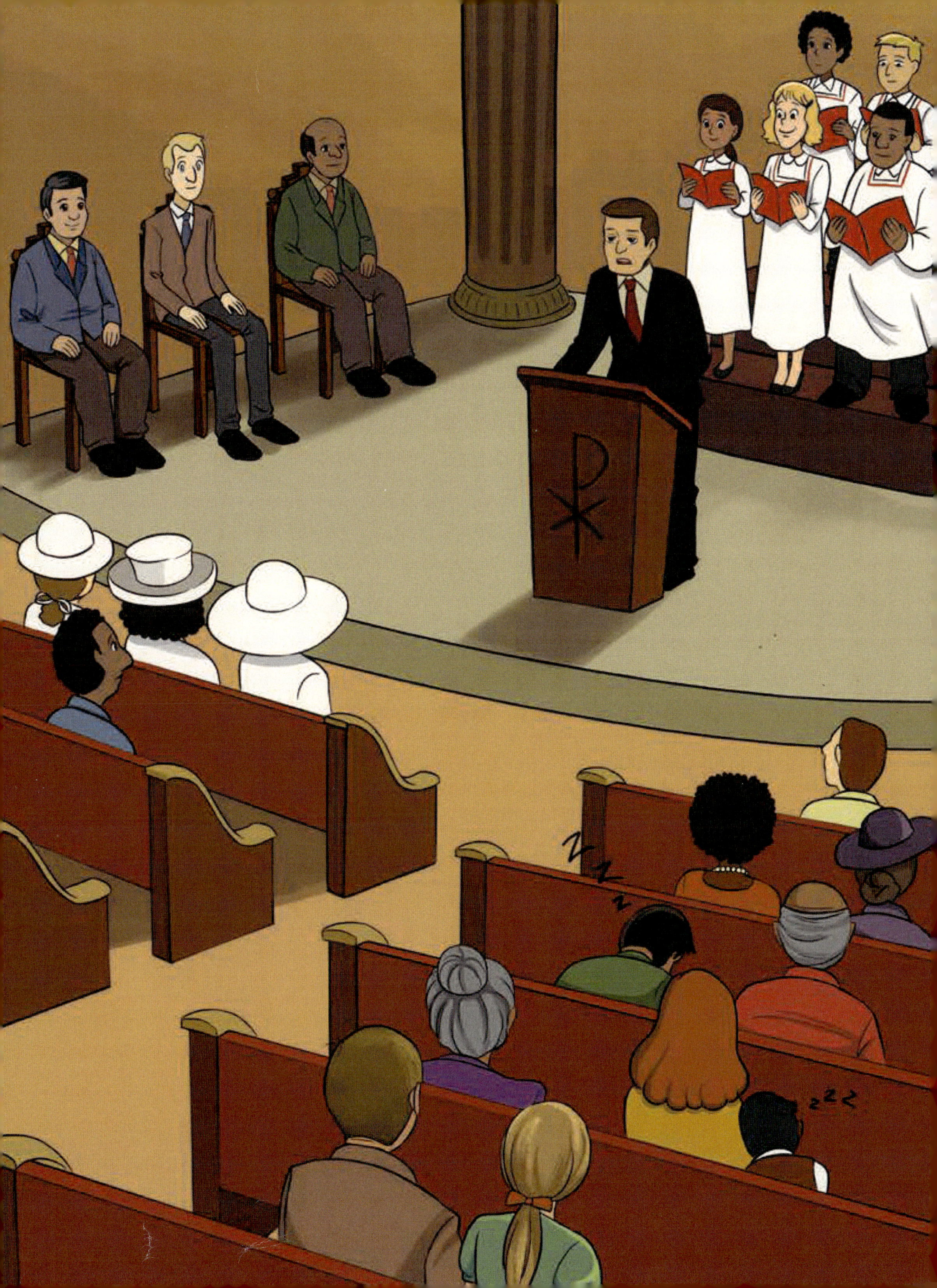

One day, in the middle of service, a frog jumped in the church.

Ribbit! Ribbit!

Right up to the preacher.

Ribbit! Ribbit!

The people went crazy!!!! They were screaming and shouting!

"Hurry and get that thang out of here. Frogs don't belong in the church," " NOT IN MY CHURCH! " said one of the deacons.

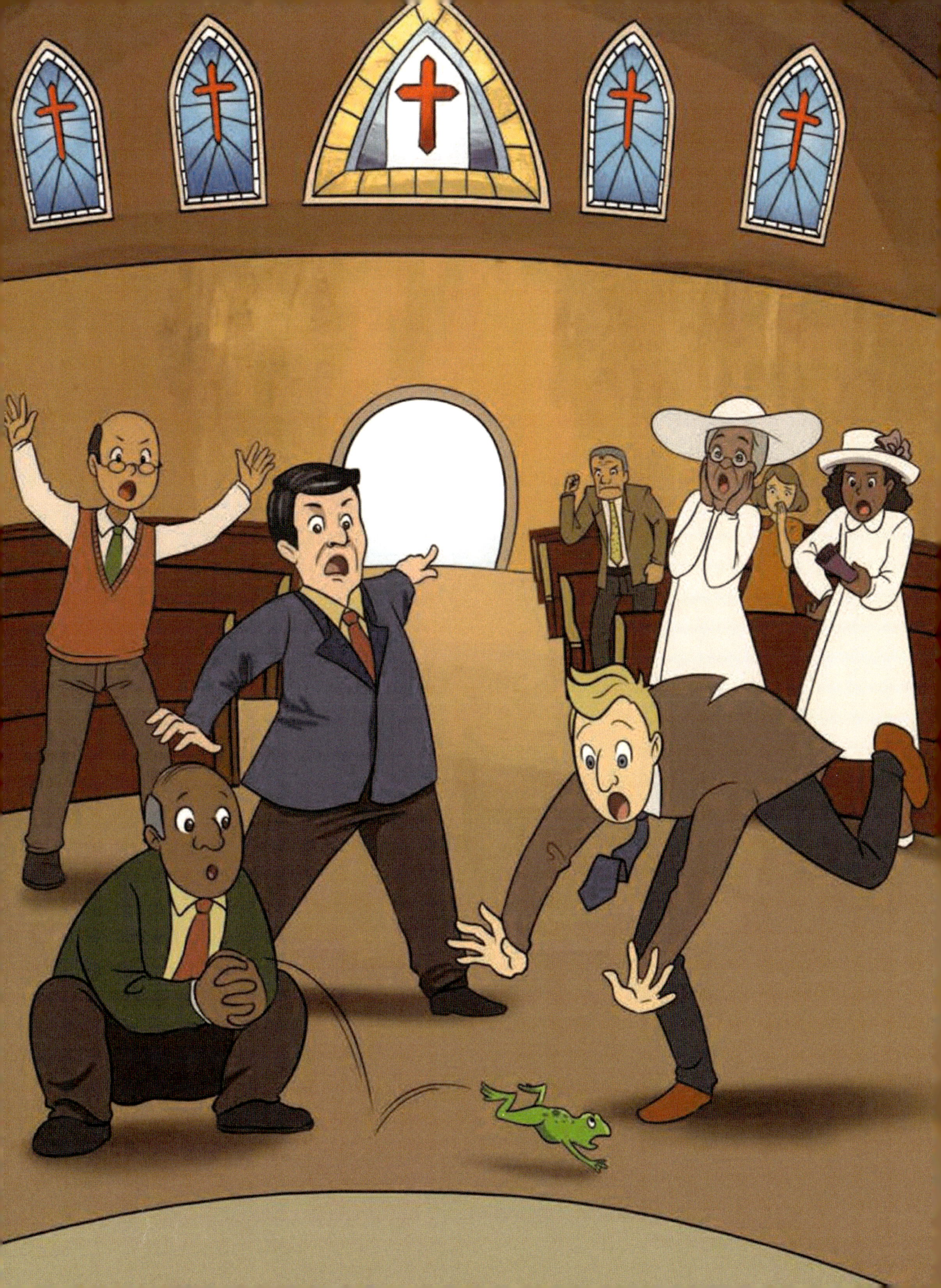

Another time, during the sermon, a bee flew into the church.

Buzzzz! Buzzzz!

All around the church,

Buzzzz! Buzzzz!

The people went bonkers! They were jumping around and waving their hands to try and catch it.

"Hurry and get that thang out of here. Bees don't belong in the church," " NOT IN MY CHURCH! " said one of the missionaries who was awakened by the bee coming in.

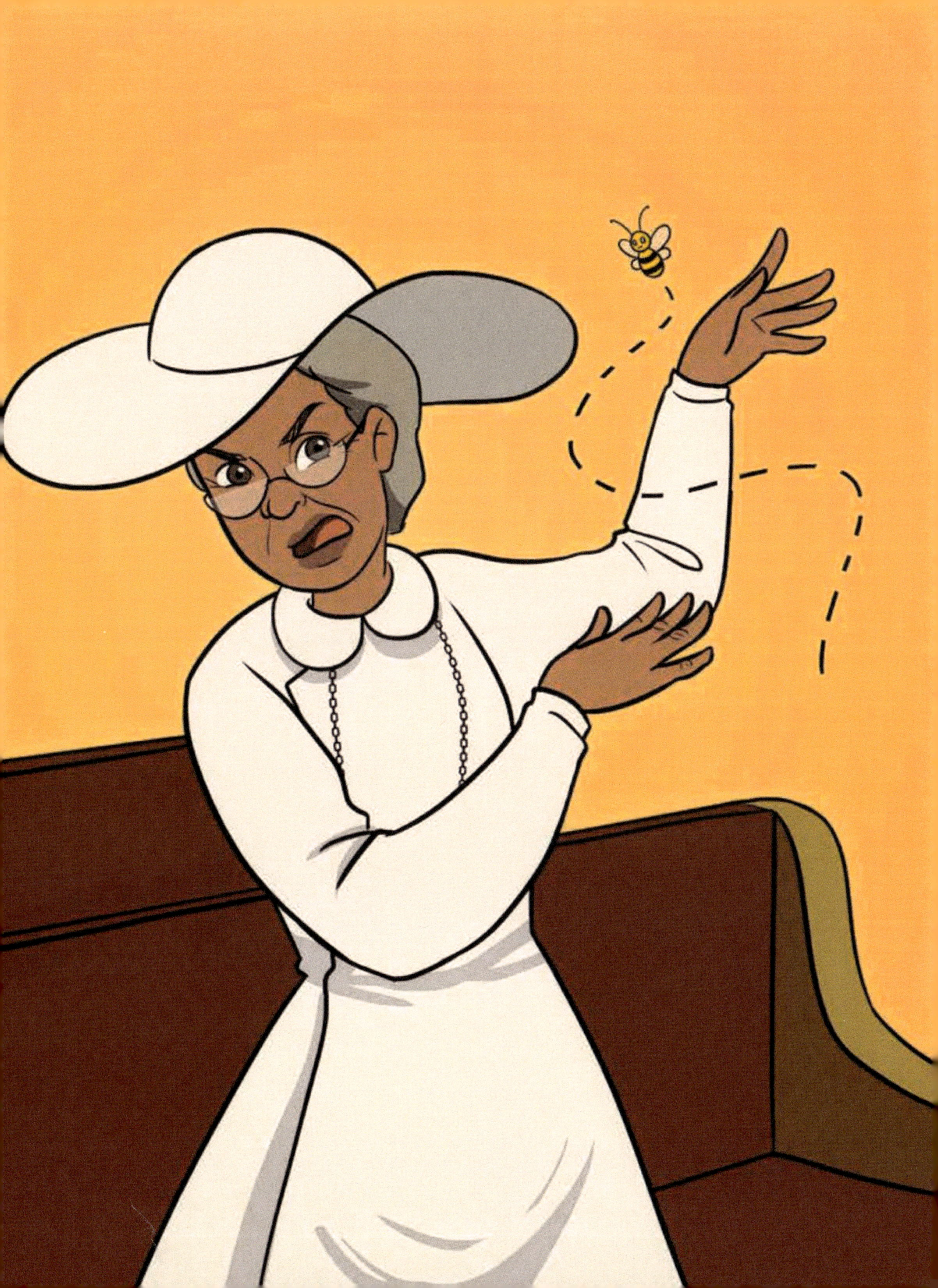

Oh and this other time, the choir was singing and a duck squawked into the church.

Quack! Quack!

Right behind the choir.

Quack! Quack!

"Hurry and get that thang out of here, Ducks don't belong in the church, " NOT IN MY CHURCH! " said one of the
choir members who really didn't want to sing anyway.

The people were getting very angry with the interruptions from the animals. "Let's close the windows and doors so these animals can't come in here anymore!" And they did just that!

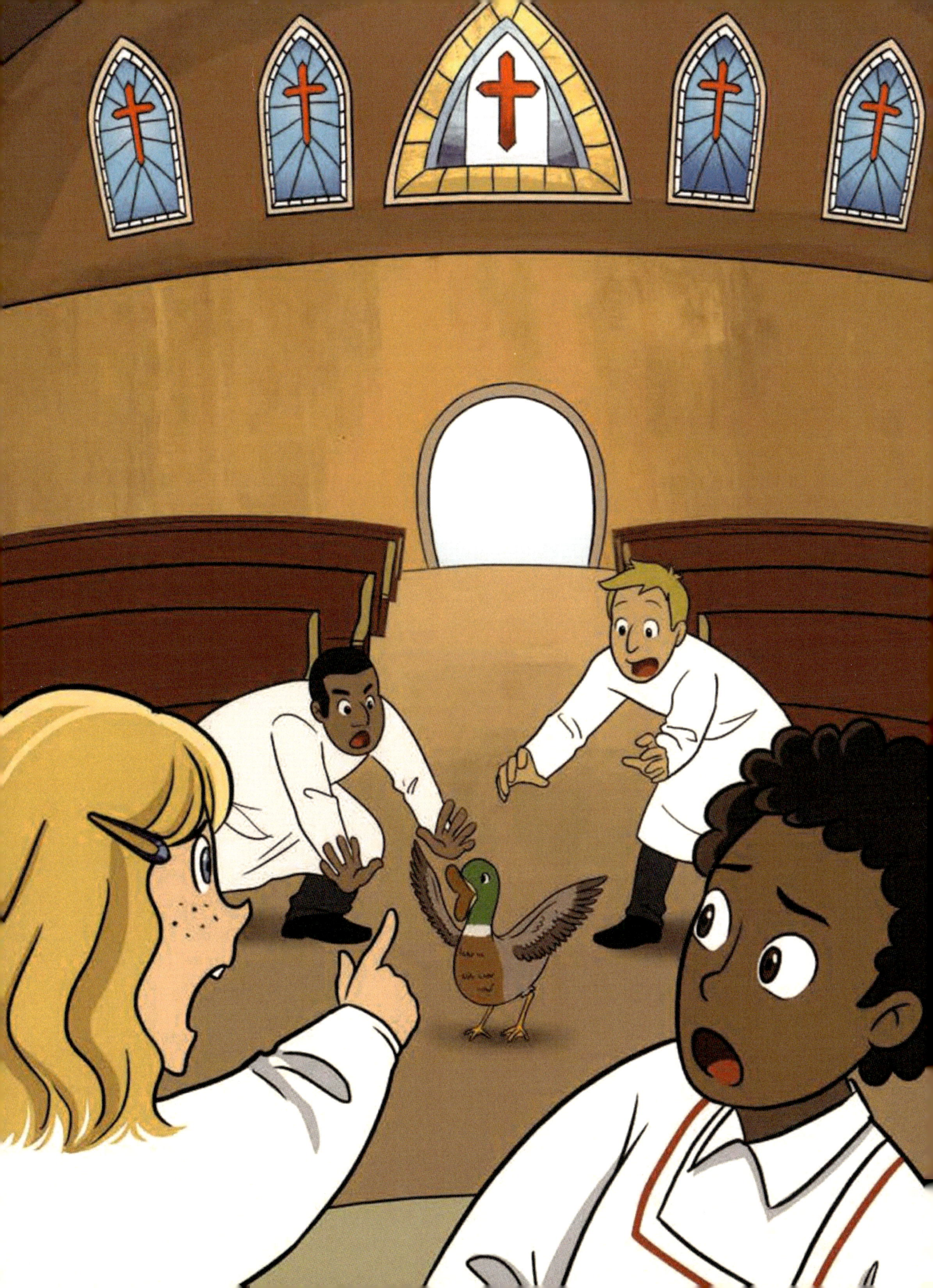

That next Sunday, from a crack in the roof, two humming-birds flew in.

Hmmm! Hmmm!

They flew all around the congregation.

Hmmm! Hmmm!

Those people didn't know what to do. They were jumping and running and waving their hands, trying get those birds out of the church.

"Hurry and get those thangs out of here. Birds don't belong in this church," " NOT IN MY CHURCH! " said one of the ministers. " I thought we handled this. I'm tired of all these interruptions!

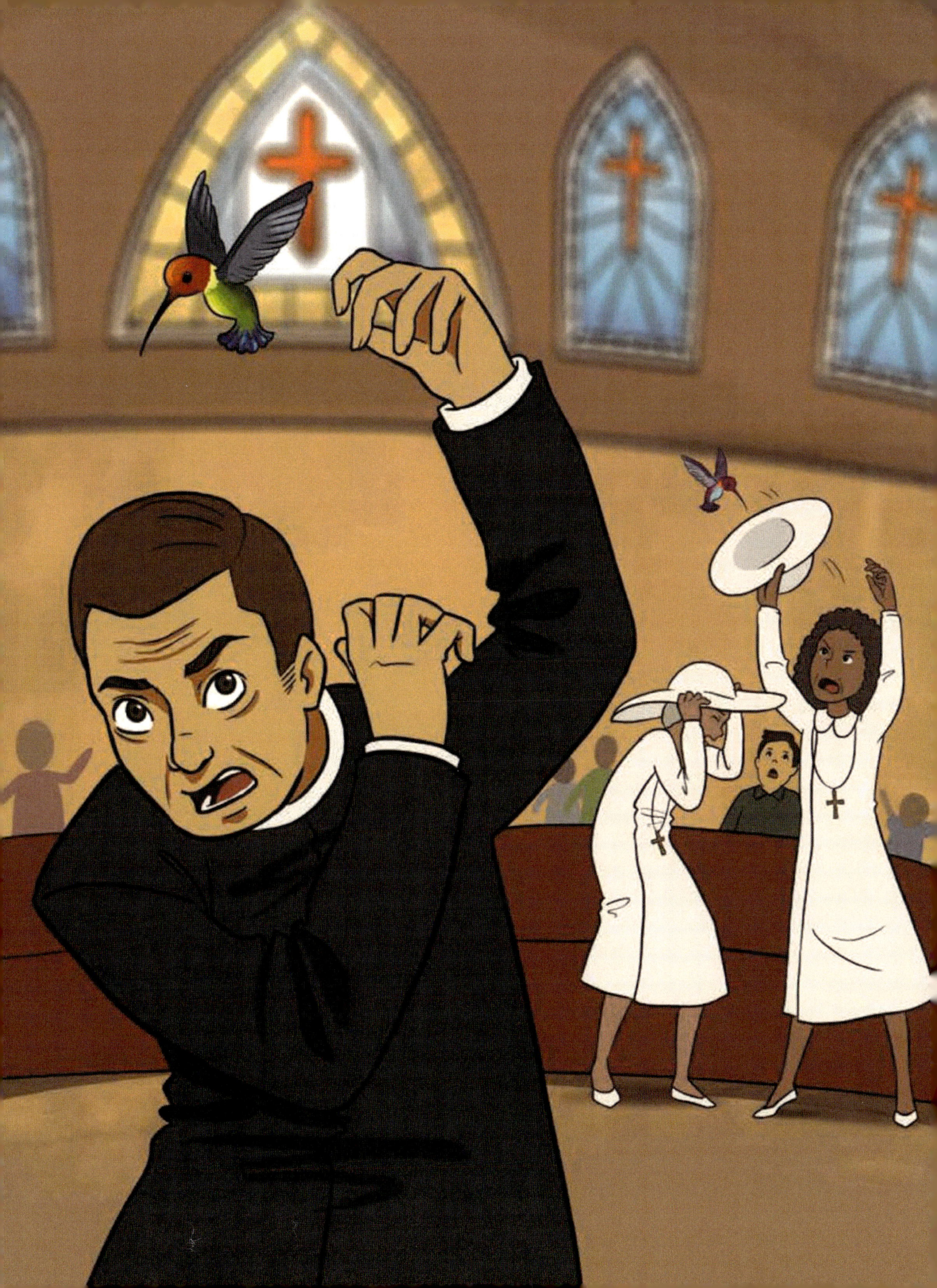

The following Sunday, those people just knew there would be no more interruptions. They closed all the windows and the doors. They sealed up any cracks in the floor and in the roof.

But some kind of way, a chicken walked in.

Bac-bac-bac-Bahkee!

Bac-bac-bac-Bahkee!

He scratched around throughout the whole congregation.

Bac-bac-bac-Bahkee!

Bac-bac-bac-Bahkee!

No one knew how he got in. They went bonkers! They were shouting and jumping and waving their hands to try to catch it.

"Hurry and get that thang out of here! He's making too much noise! Chickens don't belong in the church!" " NOT IN MY CHURCH "

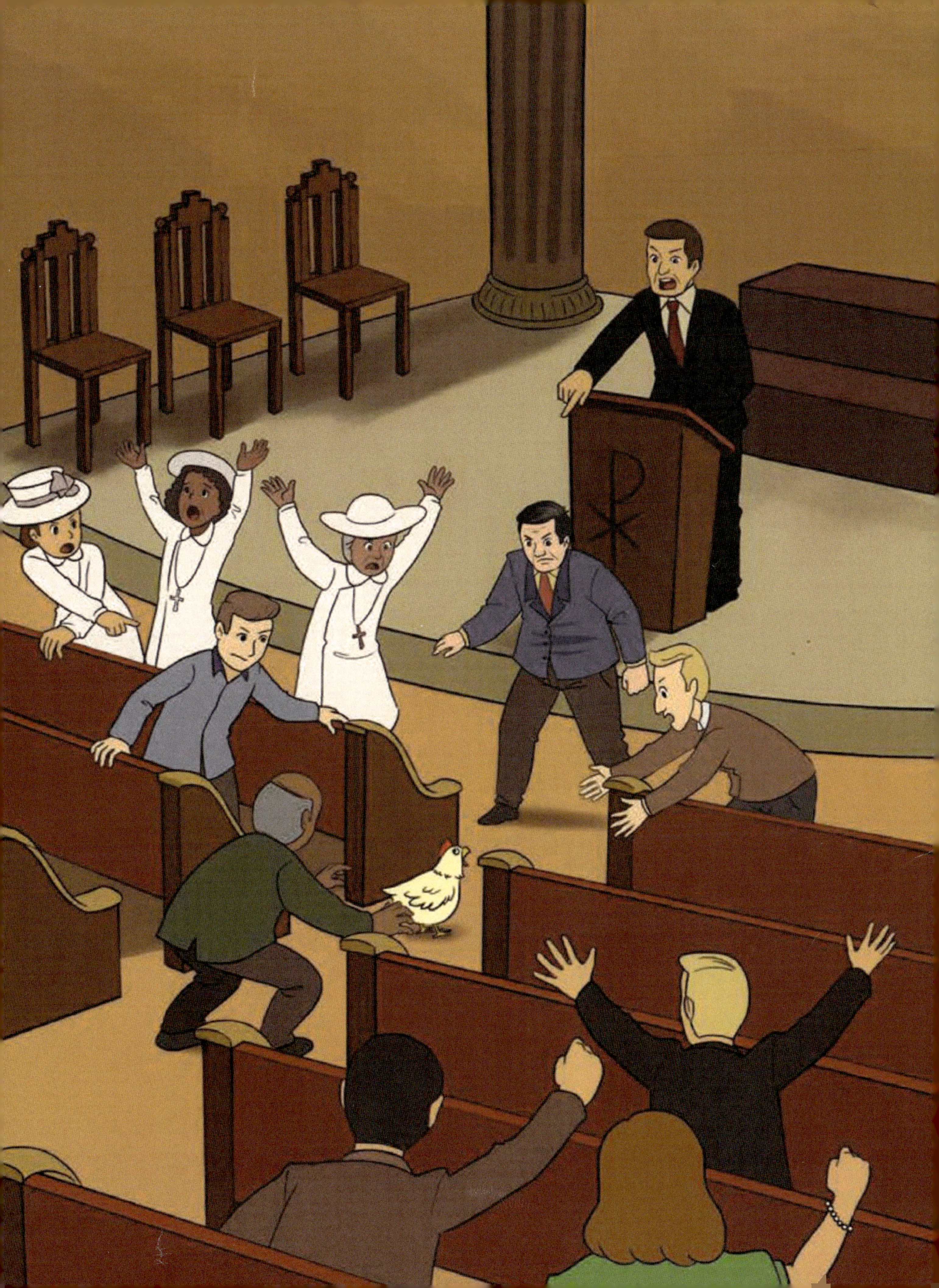

By now members were so upset! They didn't know what to do!

"We are so tired of these interruptions. They don't belong in the church, making all that racket!" They said racket instead of noise.

One day, a traveling preacher came to the church. As he sat and listened to the service, he noticed that an animal came in every time the Psalm was read. He just sat and silently giggled and prayed, "Lord, help them to see what you are trying to teach them!"

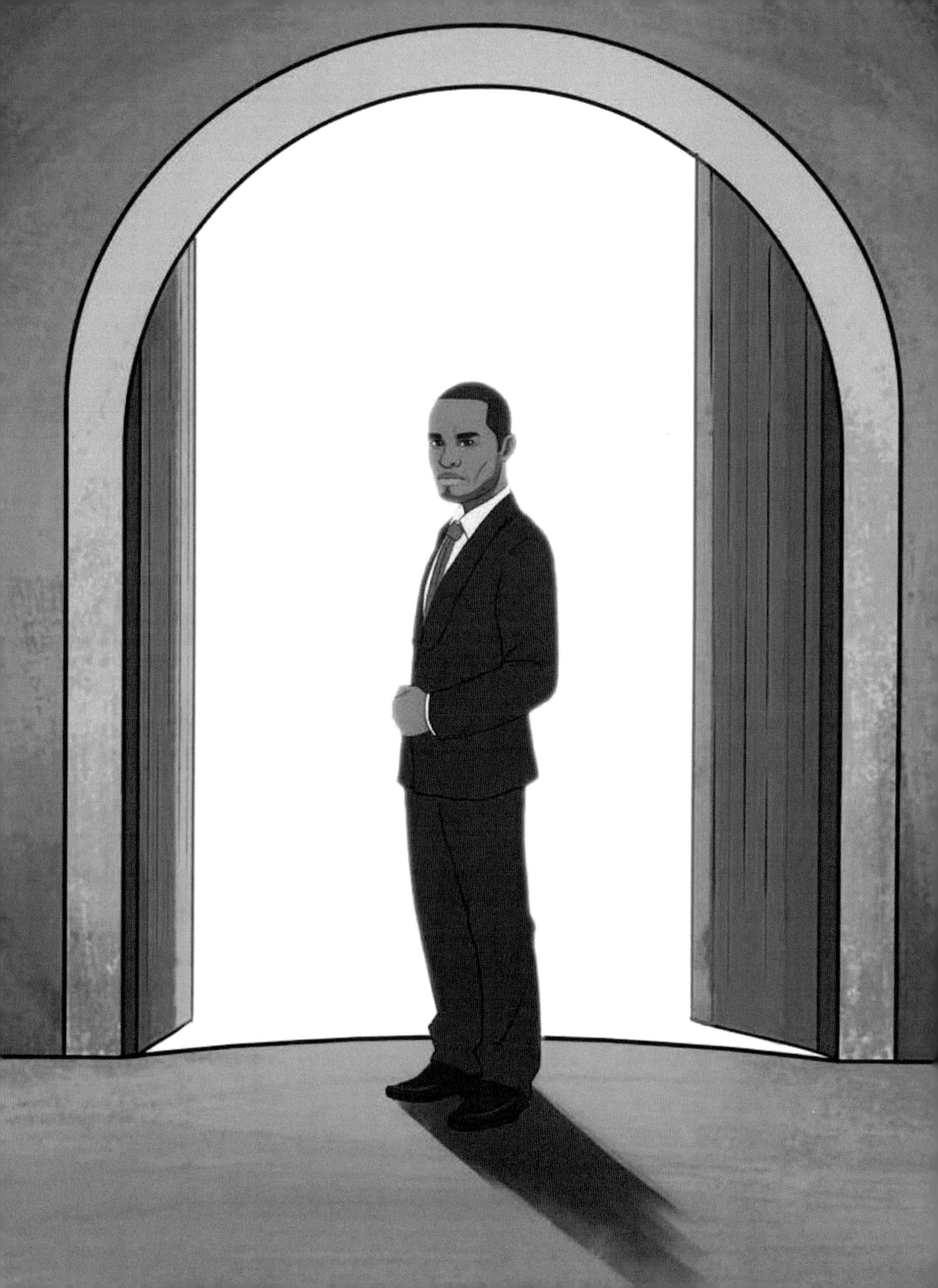

The following Sunday, it was a mess! All the animals busted into the church- the frog, the bee, the duck, the humming-birds, and the chicken.

Ribbit! Ribbit!

Bzzz, Bzzz!

Quack! Quack!

Hmmm! Hmmm!

Bac-bac-bac-Bahkee!

Bac-bac-bac-Bahkee!

The church people were as hot as fish grease, meaning they were very, very, angry! They were not used to having so much noise during church service. Church was a time for them to sit quietly and listen to the choir and the preacher, not calling out and shouting. So they all started arguing and fussing and fighting!

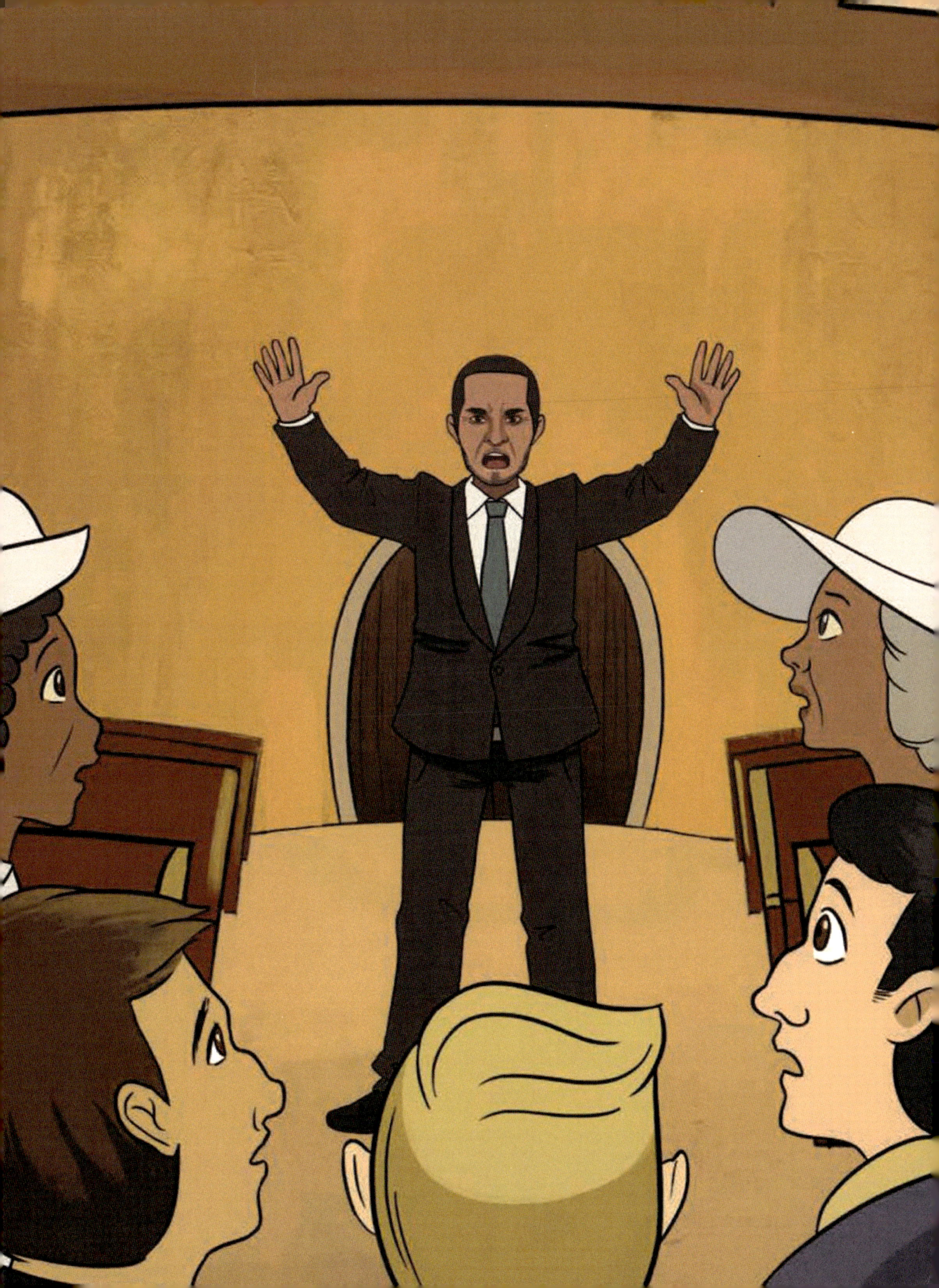

Just then the traveling preacher stood up
and shouted in a big booming preacher voice.
"Peace be still!"

Everything was quiet! You could hear a pin
drop as he started to talk.

"The Bible says if we don't praise God, the
rocks will cry out! And every week you all
read Psalm 150 and say, 'Let everything that
hath breath praise the Lord.' That's when
the animals come in. Maybe because you say
it and don't do it, God sends them to teach
you how!"

The traveling preacher taught them the many ways to praise: shouting good things about God out loud, lifting hands, running, jumping, waving hands, singing, dancing, or just saying thank you.

After he finished teaching, he read the Psalm again. Then all the people and animals praised the Lord together.

"Praise ye the Lord!"